# TRIBES of NATIVE AMERICA

Cree

edited by Marla Felkins Ryan
and Linda Schmittroth

BLACKBIRCH®
PRESS

THOMSON
★
GALE

San Diego • Detroit • New York • San Francisco • Cleveland
New Haven, Conn. • Waterville, Maine • London • Munich

# THOMSON
## GALE

Photo credits: Cover Courtesy of Northwestern University Library; cover © National Archives; cover © Photospin; cover © Perry Jasper Photography; cover © Picturequest; cover © Seattle Post-Intelligencer Collection, Museum of History & Industry; cover © PhotoDisc; cover, pages 20, 27, 31 © Library of Congress; pages 3, 8, 9, 12, 20, 24 © North Wind Archives; pages 5, 6, 7, 10, 13, 14, 17, 18, 19, 21, 22, 23, 25, 26, 28, 29, 31 © CORBIS; page 13 © Corel Corporation; pages 15, 22 © AP Wide World; page 29 © Art Resource

**LIBRARY OF CONGRESS CATALOGING-IN-PUBLICATION DATA**

Cree / Marla Felkins Ryan, book editor ; Linda Schmittroth, book editor.
    v. cm. — (Tribes of Native America)
Includes bibliographical references.
Contents: Cree name — Origins and group affiliations — History — Religion — Daily life — Festivals — Hunting rituals — Customs — Current tribal issues.
  ISBN 1-56711-690-6 (alk. paper)
  1. Cree Indians—Juvenile literature. [1. Cree Indians. 2. Indians of North America—Canada.] I. Ryan, Marla Felkins. II. Schmittroth, Linda. III. Series.
E99.C88 C73 2003
971.2004'973—dc21                                                    2002015826

**Printed in United States**
10 9 8 7 6 5 4 3 2 1

# Table of Contents

# CREE

## Name

The French called the Cree people Kristineaux. This was shortened to *Kri*, or *Cree* in English.

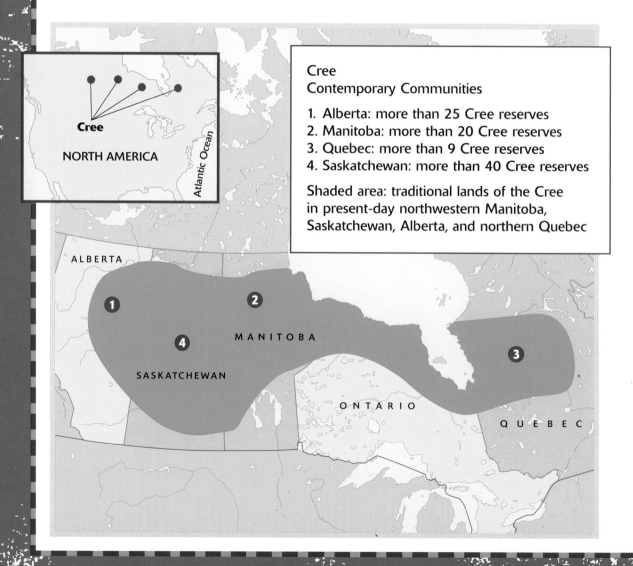

Cree

NORTH AMERICA

Atlantic Ocean

ALBERTA

MANITOBA

SASKATCHEWAN

ONTARIO

QUEBEC

Cree
Contemporary Communities

1. Alberta: more than 25 Cree reserves
2. Manitoba: more than 20 Cree reserves
3. Quebec: more than 9 Cree reserves
4. Saskatchewan: more than 40 Cree reserves

Shaded area: traditional lands of the Cree in present-day northwestern Manitoba, Saskatchewan, Alberta, and northern Quebec

## Where are the traditional Cree lands?

Canada's Cree live in an area that spans from Quebec in the east to Alberta in the west. The Plains Cree live in the parklands and plains of Alberta and Saskatchewan. The Woodland Cree live in the forests of Saskatchewan and Manitoba. A small group of Woodland Cree is called the Swampy Cree. This group lives in Manitoba, Ontario, and Quebec. American Cree are scattered throughout many states. Several hundred share the Rocky Boys Reservation in Montana with the Ojibway and other tribes.

The Cree live throughout most of the Canadian territories.

# What has happened to the population?

In the 1600s, there were about 30,000 Cree. In Canada, in 1995, there were at least 76,000 Cree. In the United States, in 1990, 8,467 people said they were Cree.

Some Cree live in Indian camps such as the one shown here in Quebec, Canada.

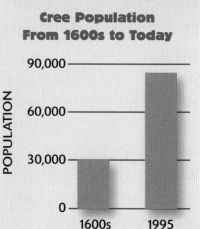

**Cree Population From 1600s to Today**

# Origins and group ties

For more than 6,000 years, Cree ancestors lived near the Arctic Circle. Some Plains Cree married French people. This created the Métis culture of the Red River Valley.

The early Cree lived in eastern Canada. They respected the animals and land that gave them what they needed. They may have been the most widespread Indian people.

In July 2000, Métis drummers performed on the front lawn of the Supreme Court of Canada in Ontario. This was part of a twenty-four-hour watch held to support a decision regarding Métis rights.

# HISTORY

## Changes come

Before they met Europeans, the Cree lived south and southwest of the Hudson Strait in northern Quebec. When English explorer Henry Hudson came in 1611, trade began between the Cree and whites. During the mid- to late 1600s, the Cree had a thriving trade in animal pelts.

The Cree traded with European settlers at stores like the Hudson Bay Company in northern Québec.

After they started to trade with Europeans, Cree trappers used guns to hunt.

## Middlemen in the fur trade

Between 1668 and 1688, the Hudson's Bay Company of England set up posts near rivers in Cree lands. Soon, the Cree became middlemen in the fur trade. They took European goods to other tribes and returned with fine furs for European traders. The Cree quickly learned white ways. They used guns to hunt and to control access to the trading posts.

Over time, the Cree went through many cultural changes. They gave up their traditional tools for those of whites. They also began to wear cloth garments instead of fur and animal skins.

The Cree traded at English posts to the north and French posts to the south. For a while, their part in the fur trade made them the richest and

**1865**
Civil War ends

**1885**
Along with the Métis, the Cree in the Saskatchewan River area fight Canadian forces in the Second Riel Rebellion

**1917–1918**
WWI fought in Europe

**1905**
Treaty No. 9 is signed at Hudson's Bay Company's Moose Factory

**1941**
Bombing at Pearl Harbor forces United States into WWII

**1945**
WWII ends

**1950s**
Reservations no longer controlled by federal government

**1971**
Quebec government plans the James Bay hydroelectroc project. Cree and Inuit protest

**1994**
James Bay II project is put on hold, largely due to the Cree's efforts

strongest tribe in the region. They paid a terrible price, though. As many as two-thirds of the Cree died after they caught white diseases to which they had no immunity.

## Many Cree move west

In the early 18th century, many Cree moved west to escape disease brought by white European settlers.

By the 1730s, many Woodland Cree wanted to escape disease epidemics and to explore new fur-hunting areas. These people moved to the Great Plains region of western Canada. Some settled as far west as the Canadian Rocky Mountains.

## Trade with Blackfeet

The Woodland Cree made an agreement with the Blackfeet, who lived on the Great Plains. The two tribes traded furs for weapons. The Cree visited the Blackfeet in spring to get furs. The Cree gave the Blackfeet weapons. Between 1790 and 1810, the Cree-Blackfeet trade agreement fell apart.

## Life on the plains grows difficult

By the mid–nineteenth century, the Plains Cree began to face problems. They moved with the buffalo herds. This meant they often intruded on the lands of other tribes and caused tensions. The buffalo had also begun to die out. Buffalo had been plentiful in 1870, but within ten years, only a few remained. Whites had killed them in huge numbers. With the buffalo gone, the tribe faced starvation.

## Attempt to become farmers

In the 1870s, the Plains Cree asked the Canadian government to help them become farmers. The government promised tools and livestock but was slow to give them. They gave the Cree plows and wagons that were barely fit for use. The Cree also were given wild cattle that could not be hitched to a plow. Still, the Cree had some success at farming.

In 1885, the Plains Cree joined the Métis in the Second Riel Rebellion. The Riel Rebellions were

In 1885, the Cree joined the Second Riel Rebellion to fight the Canadian government and protect their land rights.

among the few wars in which Canadian natives fought the government to protect their land rights. Cree chiefs Poundmaker and Big Bear led warriors against the Northwest Mounted Police (Mounties) and an army from Eastern Canada. After two major battles, the Métis gave up the fight.

## Many Plains Cree give up farming

In 1889, the Commission of Indian Affairs put a new farming system in place. It allowed each Indian farmer only one acre of wheat and a garden of roots and vegetables. The government also said the people had to use simple tools and homemade items. Many Plains Cree gave up farming entirely. Some ended up on Indian reserves (reservations), where they scratched out a meager living.

## Ontario Cree

The Cree in the East faced different challenges. In 1905, the Woodland Cree signed Treaty No. 9 at Hudson's Bay Company's Moose Factory. They were to be granted a sum of $8 when they signed and a payment of $4 every year after. In return, the Cree gave up all rights to their former land. It is not clear today whether the Cree fully understood the treaty.

Between 1920 and 1940, hundreds of Cree in Ontario died from diseases brought by whites.

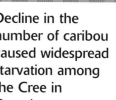

Decline in the number of caribou caused widespread starvation among the Cree in Ontario.

Starvation was also widespread due to a dramatic decline in the number of beaver and caribou that the people hunted for food. In addition, the government of Ontario began to enforce its wild game laws strictly.

The James Bay hydroelectric project flooded territory that was home to the Cree and Inuit tribes.

## Modern challenges

In 1971, the Cree in Quebec faced a new threat. The Canadian government was ready to start work on the James Bay hydroelectric project. The plan was to dam La Grande River and build stations where electricity would be produced. Cree and Inuit hunters protested this in Quebec courts. They said the project would harm their way of life. They won their case, but the decision was overturned.

# THE JAMES BAY PROJECT

In 1971, the head of the province of Quebec unveiled the James Bay Project. This $6 million hydroelectric plant was to be built near Cree lands. The project promised to create 125,000 new jobs but would also flood the rivers where the Cree hunted and trapped. For decades, the Cree and the Inuit fought the project. As they tried to stop the James Bay Project, the Cree had to prove that they had rights in the territory. They also had to prove that the project would harm those rights beyond repair.

The Cree and Inuit fought in court against development of the James Bay hydroelectric plant.

The Cree tribe of northern Quebec was made up of eight separate communities scattered across 150,000 square miles of forest. Because these communities were not organized, the fight against the government was difficult. Still, they won a court decision in their favor in 1973. A lower court ruled that the Cree and Inuit had title to their lands and that hunting was important to their way of life. The court said work on the James Bay Project would have to stop right away. Later that year, a higher court ruled that the work should go on because the project was too far along. In 1975, the Cree gave up rights to the lands involved in the power project and took a cash settlement of more than $300 million.

The first phase of the hydroelectric project was

finished in 1991. By then, one-third of the best Cree lands were underwater. Before work could begin on the next stage of the project, the Grand Council of the Cree of Quebec sued Hydro-Quebec, which ran the project.

The Cree and their supporters tried to sway public opinion against the project. They used videos and concerts, among other means, to get their message across. In the summer of 1994, the project was put on hold with no plan to start up again.

On September 30, 1991, Cree grand chief Matthew Coon Come testified before the New York state legislature against the James Bay Project.

A good deal of research has been done to determine how the project has changed the place where the Cree live. Studies found unhealthy levels of mercury in people's blood. This was the result of the building of reservoirs that affected the water supply and fish.

The grand chief of the Quebec Cree, Matthew Coon Come, explained what the James Bay Project has meant for his people: "[The dream of the hydroelectric project] has become our nightmare. It has contaminated our fish with mercury. It has destroyed the spawning grounds. It has destroyed the nesting grounds of the waterfowl. It has displaced and dislocated our people and broken the fabric of our society. And we have decided, knowing the behavior of the animals, that we will not be like the fox, who, when he sees danger, crawls back to his hole. We have come out to stop the destruction of our land."

## Religion

The Cree believed in a life force, which was similar to the Christian soul. It was found in all living beings. The Cree also believed in spirits and demons that sometimes showed up in dreams.

The Plains Cree honored one creator—the Great Manito, who controlled the whole universe. Manito was too powerful to be asked for blessings directly. Instead, he was approached by go-betweens, spirit powers called *atayohkanak*.

In the late 1880s, missionaries convinced a number of Cree to become Christians and burned the drums of Cree people. They hoped this would end Cree customs. Despite the missionaries' efforts, many Cree still hold on to their traditional beliefs.

## Government

In the Cree system of government, everyone—from chiefs to women to young people—helped make decisions. Today, a grand chief is in charge of the Grand Council of the Cree, which was founded in 1974. The tribe holds a general assembly for all Cree people in a different place each year.

## Economy

The Woodland Cree were hunters and fishermen. They trapped in winter, hunted goose in spring,

# THE SEASONS OF A CREE TRAPPER'S LIFE

Some modern-day Cree still hunt, trap, and fish to survive. Their lives are ruled by the seasons.

The trapping season runs from September through March. During that time, the men trap game, including beaver and red squirrel. April through March is hunting season. The Cree go after birds such as ducks and loons.

Some Cree still hunt, trap game, and fish to make a living.

Men who live near the coast hunt beluga whales in June and July and seals in October. Fall is the time to hunt large game, such as bear and caribou.

In winter and spring, the Cree's prey includes porcupines and rabbits. Fishing is done all year. In the summer, whole families use nets to catch whitefish, trout, and other varieties.

and fished in summer. They used bows and arrows, spears, and snares to catch game.

The Cree relied on the buffalo for many of their needs. Buffalo bones were used to make arrowheads. The tail was used as a fly swatter. Tendons were used for bowstrings and as sewing thread. Even waste material, in the form of dried dung, was burned for fuel.

# DAILY LIFE

## Families

The Cree used animal hides to build wigwams and tepees.

Men and women shared the work. Men usually hunted and carried out raids and warfare. Women performed many tasks. They prepared meat and killed beaver, and they also looked after the children.

## Buildings

The Woodland Cree lived in both cone-shaped and dome-shaped wigwams covered with bark or caribou skins. The Plains Cree used hide-covered tepees that had a three-pole foundation and a central fireplace with a smoke hole. Inside each tepee were beds made of bundles of dried grass or rushes. Buffalo robes were placed over them for warmth.

Today, most Cree live in modern homes. At their winter camps, though, woodland hunters live in *muhtukan,* rectangular-shaped houses

made of logs and sod. They also build tepee-shaped structures called *michwaup,* which are made of logs and spruce boughs.

## Clothing

Until about age five, most children wore little or no clothing. Babies were carried about in sacks lined with soft moss. The moss acted as a cushion and also served as a diaper.

During summer, men wore leather breechcloths (flaps that hung from the waist and covered the front and back). The upper body was usually left bare. Men might wear a type of poncho for ceremonies.

Women wore buffalo robes or dresses made of two oblong pieces of cloth or hide. These were

**Left:** Cree women carried their babies in bags lined with moss. **Right:** Cree men parted their hair in the center and separated it into two braids that hung in front of their shoulders.

placed one on top of the other, then sewn or laced together lengthwise.

Jewelry included earrings made of mussel shells and necklaces made of animal teeth or bones. Over time, beads and spangles bought through the Hudson's Bay Company took the place of these items.

Men plucked their facial hair. Both men and women parted their hair in the center, and formed two braids. Women tied the two braids together in back, while men tied them together in front. Some people wove in horsehair to make their hair look longer.

## Food

The Plains Cree only ate fish when hunting was poor. Buffalo was their main food, but they also hunted moose, caribou, and other game.

The most commonly eaten root was the turnip. It was cooked many ways and even eaten raw. Berries were often added to dried meat. The first berries of the season were eaten only after each family had held its own ritual feast.

When food was in short supply, the people gathered algae, fungus, and caribou dung. They boiled and ate these items.

The Cree diet included a variety of roots, berries, fish, and meat.

## Education

Cree children were never beaten and were rarely scolded. Ties between grandparents and their grandchildren were very close. Elders helped young people learn to make big decisions about life.

During the early 20th century, the Anglican Church in Canada ran elementary schools in some Cree communities. Cree children who had been educated at home in their early years often had trouble in the new schools. At Canadian boarding schools, they were expected to adopt white ways

The Cree language is now available in places where the tribe has formed its own school boards.

The Cree used certain plants to treat wounds and illnesses.

and were not allowed to speak their native language.

The Cree School Board was created in the late 1970s to help make education fit Cree needs. Today, each Cree community in Quebec runs its own school under the management of the Cree School Board. Many children now study the Cree language in their schools.

## Healing practices

Healers called shamans (pronounced *SHAH-munz* or *SHAY-munz*) were well respected within the tribe. They were seen as links between the human and animal worlds. They could cure illnesses and do magic.

A tribe often had several shamans. Shamans used dreams and rituals to contact the spirit world. The Cree believed that evil shamans could bring disease or misfortune upon victims if they chose.

The Cree practiced bloodletting (opening a vein to drain blood) to cure the sick. They also knew how to set broken bones. Knowledge of healing plants was usually passed down through families or bought from other Indians.

# CUSTOMS

## Names

Children were named by a shaman at around age one. The shaman chose a name based on a vision. During the naming ceremony, the baby was passed from person to person. Each one called the child by its new name and wished it future happiness.

## Vision quests

During puberty, a Cree boy took part in the vision quest. This rite put him in touch with the spirit who would guide him through life. He was taught a special song, then went with his father to a secluded spot. The boy wore nothing but his breechcloth. He covered himself with white clay and built a brush shelter. The father then made a pipe offering to the spirits and left the boy alone. The boy often did feats of endurance to try to bring on a vision. After he went back to camp, he described his vision to others.

Cree babies were named by the tribal shaman.

At the beginning of puberty, young Cree women were sent to live in a tepee outside of their village for four nights.

## Female coming of age ceremony

At the time of a Cree girl's first menstruation, she was secluded for four nights in a small tepee outside the village. An old woman told her stories and taught her about the duties of an adult woman. The girl was kept very busy. She chopped wood, sewed, and tanned hides. It was while she worked that she was most likely to have a vision. After her fourth and final night in seclusion, a feast was held in her honor.

## The Sun Dance

The most important of the Plains Indian ceremonies, the Sun Dance, was called the All-Night-Thirst-Dance by the Plains Cree. During the whole four-day ceremony, the people involved drank nothing.

Sun Dancers once engaged in a bloody rite. They pierced their skin with a sharp buffalo horn threaded with a leather thong. The thong was tied to a pole or the rafters of a building. As they danced, the people tore themselves free from the poles, and offered pieces of their flesh to the god Manito.

Some groups did not do this. Instead, they danced without food or water for four days and gazed at the sun. They swayed back and forth until they were so tired that they fainted. In a modern form of the ritual, dancers stand behind green leaves and bend their knees as they blow a whistle. As the sun beats down on them, they stare at one spot on the center pole and do not eat or drink.

Plains Cree participated in All-Night-Thirst-Dances as an offering to the god Manito.

## Shaking Tent Ceremony

Another important ceremony was the Shaking Tent Ceremony. In it, a shaman prayed and purified himself in a sweat lodge, then stripped to his breechcloth. He was bound with leather thongs and hung up inside the tent. The spirits were supposed to free him.

When the spirits came, the tent began to shake. Sounds could be heard from inside. Listeners could hear a conversation between the spirits and the shaman. Then, the leather thongs that tied the shaman would shoot out from the top of the tent.

Cree children had to join a Walking Out ceremony before they were allowed to cross the thresholds of their homes by themselves.

## Walking Out Ceremony

Young Cree children were not allowed to cross the threshold of their home by themselves until they had taken part in a Walking Out ceremony. At dawn on the day of the ritual, family and friends gathered with the village toddlers in a large tent. Each child crossed the threshold with his or her parents or grandparents and went outside. The group followed a path to a tree about 20 feet away. The child made a circle around the tree, then went back to the tent. The child was now an official member of the tribe.

## The Grass Dance

The most common ceremony on Cree reservations today is the Grass Dance, or Warrior's Dance. In this ritual, bundles of braided grass are tied to the dancers' belts. These symbolize scalps. In the 1940s, when many Cree men left home to fight in World War II (1939–1945), women kept the dance alive.

## Sweat baths and passing pipes

Sweat lodges were used for ceremonial cleansing and for pleasure. Inside the lodge, water was poured on hot stones to produce a refreshing steam.

To begin all rituals and social occasions, the Cree shared a pipe. Men passed the pipe in a clockwise direction. They believed that the gods smoked along with the men and listened to any requests made during the ceremony.

Cree Indians developed hunting rituals. In this 1927 photograph, a Cree man blows a horn to call a moose as part of a hunting ritual.

## Hunting rituals

In the Cree's view, the gods had given animals to them. Animals made their own decisions whether to take part in the hunt. In return for the animals' agreement to be hunted, hunters made sure animals could grow and survive on the earth.

Plains Indian tribes sometimes still wear traditional costumes and dance in ceremonies.

To hunt buffalo, the Cree drove them into places where they would stumble—snowdrifts in winter or marshes in summer. Then, the herd was stampeded into a corral-like structure and shot with arrows.

## War rituals and raids

When a man went to war, he took with him a sacred bundle that held one piece of war equipment. These bundles were thought to have magical properties. Often, a warrior was stripped of his belongings when he returned to the village. Even the horses he took in raids were given to relatives and friends.

For the Plains Cree, warfare was done not to conquer other tribes, but to win honor by counting coup (pronounced coo). The warrior rode up to an

Some Cree drew hunting, ritual dance, and battle scenes on clothing made from buffalo hides.

armed enemy and touched him with a type of stick. Four coups were enough to make someone a chief. Ranking among chiefs depended upon their war exploits.

## Courtship and marriage

Women usually married three to four years after their first menstruation. Men married at around age 25. High-ranking men often had two or more wives.

Parents usually chose their children's mates. A young woman's father would give a gift to the young man he thought was a good match. If the young man's parents approved, they set up a new tepee for the couple. The bride sat inside, then the groom entered the tent and sat beside her. The bride gave him a new pair of moccasins. If he took them, the marriage was sealed.

Cree brides gave their grooms moccasins as part of the wedding ceremony. If the shoes were accepted, the marriage was official.

## Funerals

When a person died, his or her close relatives dressed only in robes and let their hair loose. They cut gashes in their skin to show their grief. The property of the deceased was given away but not often to family members. The dead were placed in a grave about five feet deep and lined with a robe.

In June 2002, chairman of the Chippewa Cree Tribe Business Committee, Alvin Windy Boy, spoke to a group of tribal leaders about health problems on Indian reservations.

## Current tribal issues

Modern Cree face many problems. As they have adopted European and American ways, they have lost many of their traditions and beliefs. They also have high rates of alcoholism and suicide.

Vandalism and family violence are other problems that continue to arise.

In the 1990s, the Cree dealt with several matters that concerned their relations with the Quebec government. They discussed forestry development and its impact on the environment. Tribal people hope to protect their way of life, and to be able to use their lands as they see fit.

# Notable people

Buffy Sainte-Marie (c. 1942– ) is a well-known folksinger and an Academy Award-winning songwriter, as well as an advocate for Indian rights.

Chief Poundmaker (c. 1842–1886) took part in the Métis rebellion against the Canadian government in 1885. He was convicted of treason, served a term in prison, and died shortly after his release.

Other notable Cree include head chief and resistance leader Big Bear (c. 1825–1888); Payepot, 19th century leader of the Western Canadian Plains Cree; painter and illustrator Jackson Beardy (1944–1984); and tribal leader Harold Cardinal (1945– ).

Cree folk singer Buffy Sainte-Marie is an Indian rights activist.

# For More Information

Erdoes, Richard. *The Sun Dance People: The Plains Indians, Their Past and Present.* New York: Random House, 1972.

Flannery, Regina. *Ellen Smallboy: Glimpses of a Cree Woman's Life.* Montreal: McGill-Queens University Press, 1995.

*Grand Council of the Cree* web site: http://gcc.ca

Cree chief Poundmaker participated in the 1885 Métis rebellion.

# Glossary

**Raid** an attack on land or on a settlement, usually to steal food and other goods

**Reserve** Canadian name for a reservation

**Reservation** land set aside and given to Native Americans

**Ritual** something that is a custom or done in a certain way

**Treaty** an agreement

**Tribe** a group of people who live together in a community

# Index

971.2004 Cree.
C

$23.70                    YPXZ021270

| DATE | | | |
|------|------|------|------|
|      |      |      |      |
|      |      |      |      |
|      |      |      |      |
|      |      |      |      |
|      |      |      |      |
|      |      |      |      |
|      |      |      |      |
|      |      |      |      |
|      |      |      |      |
|      |      |      |      |
|      |      |      |      |
|      |      |      |      |
|      |      |      |      |
|      |      |      |      |